Becoming Mentally Tougher In Bodybuilding by Using Meditation:

Reach Your Potential by Controlling Your Inner Thoughts

By

Joseph Correa

Certified Meditation Instructor

COPYRIGHT

© 2016 Finibi Inc

All rights reserved

Reproduction or translation of any part of this work beyond that permitted by section 107 or 108 of the 1976 United States Copyright Act without the permission of the copyright owner is unlawful.

This publication is designed to provide accurate and authoritative information in regard to the subject matter covered. It is sold with the understanding that neither the author nor the publisher is engaged in rendering medical advice. If medical advice or assistance is needed, consult with a doctor. This book is considered a guide and should not be used in any way detrimental to your health. Consult with a medical professional before starting any of the meditation or visualization practices shown here to make sure they are right for you.

ACKNOWLEDGEMENTS

To my friends and family who have motivated me to always reach for my dreams.

Becoming Mentally Tougher In Bodybuilding by Using Meditation:

Reach Your Potential by Controlling Your Inner Thoughts

By

Joseph Correa

Certified Meditation Instructor

CONTENTS

Copyright

Acknowledgments

About the Author

Introduction

What is Meditation?

CHAPTER 1: HOW WILL MEDITATION BENEFIT YOU?

CHAPTER 2: HOW CAN BODYBUILDERS BENEFIT FROM MEDITATING?

CHAPTER 3: THE BEST TYPES OF MEDITATION FOR BODYBUILDING

CHAPTER 4: HOW TO PREPARE TO MEDITATE

CHAPTER 5: PERFORMANCE ENHANCING BREATHING PATTERNS ALL BODYBUILDERS SHOULD LEARN IN ORDER TO MEDITATE

CHAPTER 6: DIET AND MEDITATION FOR BODYBUILDING

CHAPTER 7: THE POWER OF USING VISUALIZATIONS FOR BODYBUILDING

CHAPTER 8: MEDITATING FOR MAXIMUM BODYBUILDING RESULTS

CHAPTER 9: MEDITATING FOR EMOTIONAL STRENGTH

CHAPTER 10: MEDITATING FOR MENTAL TOUGHNESS

CHAPTER 11: MEDITATING FOR PROBLEM SOLVING

FINAL COMMENTS

MORE TITLES BY THIS AUTHOR

ABOUT THE AUTHOR

As a certified meditation instructor, I am a firm believer in the power that can be harnessed from the mind.

Having performed as a professional athlete, I understand what goes through your mind and how nerves and pressure can affect your performance.

The three biggest changes in my life have come from switching from a weight training environment to a more nutrition based, flexibility improved, and **mentally focused environment** which have had a significant change in my performance and in my life.

Meditation and visualization have helped me control my emotions and simulate live competitions before they even happened.

Adding yoga and extended periods of stretching have reduced my injuries to almost zero and have improved my reaction and speed.

Improving my nutrition has more than allowed me to continue performing at my peak under difficult climatic conditions which might have affected me in the past causing cramps and muscle pulls.

Becoming Mentally Tougher In Bodybuilding by Using Meditation

By far, meditation and visualization will change everything no matter what athletic discipline you're in. You will see how powerful it is once you spend more and more time on it and dedicate a minimum of 10 minutes a day to breathing, focused thinking, and concentrating.

My knowledge and continued practice of meditation and visualization has helped me live healthier and stronger throughout the years, which has benefitted me in all aspects of life. The more you use your brain to develop yourself and all that you can obtain, the more you will want to continue practicing meditation and visualization.

Unlock your true potential by learning and practicing meditation and visualization starting right now!

INTRODUCTION

Meditation is one of the best ways to reach your true potential. Eating right and training are two of the pieces of the puzzle but you need the third piece to reach your true potential. The third piece is mental toughness and that can be obtained through meditation.

Bodybuilders who practice meditation regularly will find they are or have:

- More confident during competition.
- Reduced stress levels.
- Better capacity to concentrate for long periods for time.
- Lower muscle fatigue.
- Faster recovery times after competing or training.
- Overcome nervousness better.
- Control their emotions under pressure.

What more can you ask for as a bodybuilder?

When considering unlocking their true potential most athletes focus on physical and nutritional goals but often overlook their inner potential through practices like meditation and visualization. It's common to want to see physical benefits from physical exercises but what many athletes don't know is that meditation has been proven to improve physical health and performance.

Reaching your peak performance requires that you train and stimulate the body and mind. Not taking this into account may be the main reason why some athletes have trouble getting to the next level. In order to do your best you must accept that the body and the mind are what will make you complete.

Meditation as exercise for the mind helps to strengthen your mind as you would strengthen your body, consistently evolving as you practice it.

Physical conditioning, good nutrition, and meditation are the three keys to achieve a state of optimal performance. Most athletes don't pay as much attention to meditation as they should because their mostly worried about appearance and how others perceive them.

Results, in meditation, are not something you will see physically but rather in how you feel and in your new ability to control your thoughts and emotions. By starting your meditation sessions and being disciplined and consistent you will notice significant improvements in how you respond to anxiety, pressure, and stress which are three of the major issues most athletes have trouble overcoming in life and when trying to reach their true potential.

Change your life and start using meditation to surpass your limits and break free!

WHAT IS MEDITATION?

Meditation is a state of mind where you are reflecting or thinking about something with a calm mind. Meditation and normal thinking are two different things. When meditating you are achieving a much higher state of concentration where nothing is clouding your mind and interacting with your thoughts.

Mediation requires much more concentration and that's why it's so important to be in a distraction free environment where external noises won't interrupt your focus.

Your normal thoughts may last for a few seconds but in meditation those thoughts and the relaxation process is meant to last from 5 minutes to however long you want.

Thoughts can be many but when meditating you hyper focus on one thought at a time. Sometimes when meditating you might just focus on having a clear mental state.

Meditation can be used for religious or non-religious purposes but in this book it will be used for non-religious purposes only.

You can use meditation at any time during the day or at night when you feel you need to calm yourself down and find a state of feeling more mentally balanced.

As you become more advanced at meditation you will move into this state of mind quicker because you will get better at blocking out distractions, and this will allow you to center your mind much sooner.

In meditation you want to zone out negative interfering thoughts, stressful situations, or any interrupting factors when you're trying to reach a state of much higher and deeper focus on any ideas you are working to concentrate on.

To maximize your potential you will need to be able to quiet the mind and leave any mental distractions behind and let your mind surpass any obstacles in the way.

CHAPTER 1: HOW WILL MEDITATION BENEFIT YOU?

The benefits of meditation can be broken down to physical benefits, mental benefits, emotional benefits, and spiritual benefits as you will see.

It doesn't matter if you are tall, short, smart, or slow, meditation is for anyone who wants to improve themselves.

I find that emotionally, meditation is wonderful but everyone is different and you might find it to benefit one aspect of your life more than others.

Meditation has been shown to help anxiety, reduction and since anxiety and stress are some of the most serious mental issues affecting athletes around the world, this is an important topic. Meditation prevents overall progress of stress and anxiety to better overcome it and eliminate it as much as possible from our lives.

In fact, meditation is on the best ways to control stress and reduce health problems that arise due to stress. Stress can cause lack of sleep and a reduction of energy levels which will affect your attitude, performance at work, patience, and tolerance.

Meditation is one of the greatest stress controlling techniques around, so you can easily start adding it to your life and begin feeling healthier and better on a day to day basis.

Physical Benefits

When most athletes think of something granting physical benefits, their thoughts tend to be on some form of physical exercise. This might include exercises like: running, biking, swimming, walking, and weight training. It's normal to think of physical exercises as a solution to improve your physical health but physical benefits can come about in different ways and meditation proves this.

Some of the physical improvements that can be seen after meditating are:

1. **Your ability to reduce your heart rate** to help you control your emotions better. Stress and anxiety have a tendency to increase your heart rate. Being able to control this will be very beneficial if you're under pressure constantly.

2. **Your ability to reduce your blood pressure.** Besides lowing your heart rate, meditation will also help you with lowing your blood pressure. High blood pressure levels equate to a much greater risk of heart disease and stroke. Too many things in our environment, especially

food, easily raise your blood pressure. Having a powerful tool like meditation on your side will assist you in overcoming this.

3. **Your ability to control muscular tension.** Athletes who have tight muscles usually will be more prone to muscular imbalances and can have muscle tears much more often than people who have learned to relax their muscles. Athletes will recover much faster and feel less fatigued after meditating. When you reduce muscle tension, your muscles will recover faster due to the improved quality of rest which will only improve physical performance. For athletes who compete at high levels, you don't want to overlook this benefit.

4. **Your ability to stay calm under stressful situations.** Being able to control your emotions better will help you to stay calm when things don't go the way you planned them to or when things get stressful.

5. **Your improved approach towards anxiety and fear.** Most athletes find themselves worrying less and being less afraid to do things after they have been able to think things through in their mind first. This will better prepare you and make you feel more confident.

6. **Your ability to strengthen your immune system.** Being less stressed out, less worried, having lower blood pressure levels, and resting better will all account for an improved immune system that will help you feel stronger, healthier, and more energetic than ever before.

7. **Enhanced ability to recover after physical training.** Meditation can help to strengthen the immune system response time, and this in turn can help you recover faster from workout sessions that you are doing. If your immune system, is weak, as is normal for become who are constantly under pressure, in a rush, and seriously stressed out, this can make you feel tired which makes it harder to bounce back after a workout session is completed. By practicing meditation on a daily basis, you will see a faster increase in your rate of recovery so that you can be ready sooner and get back to training again with more energy.

These were some of the most common physical benefits that you will see and feel from practicing meditation. You will notice meditation requires little or no movement at all, but don't think that it won't influence you in a physical way.

Mental Benefits

As you can imagine, the mental or psychological benefits of meditation tend to be even more powerful as this is largely a mentally-focused form of practice.

Some of the primary mental benefits of meditation are:

1. **Improved approach towards anger.** Some athletes tend to get angry very easily, sometimes for no reason at all. The first mental benefit you will see is a reduced level of anger and aggression. Because you will feel more in control over your emotions. You will be less likely to let your emotions get the best of you. For those that tend to be very aggressive on a daily basis, you can use meditation to calm these feelings down when they start to get out of hand.

2. **Improved capacity to concentrate.** Meditation can help you to focus for much longer periods of time and will allow you to make these, high quality concentration periods. THIS IS ONE OF THE GREATEST BENEFITS YOU CAN OBTAIN FROM MEDITATING and one that should not be overlooked. Being able to block out distractions and stay focused on the task at hand can be a major obstacle that meditation will help you overcome.

3. **Greater confidence in yourself.** Athletes who regularly perform meditation often say they feel more confident. Self-confidence comes from feeling you have greater control over specific events in your life. When you have more self-esteem, it will show in everything you do, whether it's interacting with others or when trying to reach your goals. Meditation can make you feel empowered and strong. For most athletes, the reduction in stress alone is enough motivation to keep them practicing meditation on a daily basis.

4. **You'll feel more relaxed.** The process of breathing and closing your eyes combined with focused thinking will help you feel calmer and more relaxed.

We won't go over the spiritual benefits of meditation in this book but you may research this topic if you are interested in further learning more about this topic.

CHAPTER 2: HOW CAN BODYBUILDERS BENEFIT FROM MEDITATING?

Meditation can be used by athletes for different reasons: stress, anxiety, concentration, nerves, etc. Athletes can benefit from meditation by seeing a faster rate of recovery which is fundamental when trying to push yourself to the next level of performance. Training sessions will be more intense and of higher quality due to the improved level of concentration and due to the reduction of fatigue in their muscles. Most athletes will see a reduction in nervousness before and during competition which will help them compete better and more confidently.

Once you start practicing on a regular basis you will find that you have increased capacity to concentrate and focus, when it comes time to perform under pressure and under unexpected conditions. This increased capacity to focus will take you to an even higher level of performance.

Athletes with risk of heart disease can benefit significantly from meditation. Doctors are now prescribing more meditation and less medication which is common sense for some and life changing for others. By simply reducing the amount of stress an athlete is exposed to on a daily basis will reduce blood pressure levels and improve their competitiveness by being able to take on more training. Some athletes have found that meditation can often help control stress eating which is not commonly talked about but a significant factor that steers people away from reaching their peak performance. Athletes often find they are more in control of their lives after repeating meditation sessions often which reduces stress and as a direct benefit, lowers the risk of heart disease.

Weight loss is a common problem because of not having proper planning and not being able to follow diets because of lack of discipline or poor habits. MEDITATION CAN ACTUALLY HELP WITH WEIGHT LOSS TO HAPPEN when overeating is due to stress.

Athletes trying to break bad habits will find it difficult to change their old ways and start on a new path. Smoking, drinking alcohol, nervousness, getting angry, and other negative habits can be controlled through meditation as it can reduce cravings. Slowing things down and using breathing techniques to focus on overcoming bad habits when meditating can be a powerful technique that seems less obvious but more relevant when bad habits have been developed due to stress and anger.

Athletes who suffer from depression or anxiety also suffer from stress as it is a major contributor towards the first two. Negative health states can be dramatically improved through the practice of meditation on a regular basis. When you practicing meditation you will notice it easier for you to have more control over your mood and will feel more positive about the future in general. Many athletes worry too much about the outcome or past failed outcomes which are irrelevant to the present if you take the time to maximize your present potential through improved nutrition and meditation. If your goal is to control your thoughts and emotions better, you will find that meditating will calm you down and allow you not to feel overwhelmed under strenuous situations.

CHAPTER 3: THE BEST TYPES OF MEDITATION FOR BODYBUILDING

Mindfulness

During mindfulness, athletes should be trying to stay in the present in each and every thought that they currently have entering their mind.

This type of meditation teaches you to become aware of your breathing patterns, but doesn't attempt to change them in any way through breathing practices. This is a more passive form of meditation compared to other more active forms of meditation which will require you to change your breathing patterns. Mindfulness is one of the most common types of meditation in the world and one that all athletes can greatly benefit from.

Focused meditation

Athletes using meditation are directing their thoughts to a specific problem, emotion, or object they want to focus on and find a solution for.

Begin by clearing your mind of all distractions and then taking some time to focus on just a single sound, object, or thought. You are trying to focus for as long as possible in this state of mind where you can then redirect your concentration to an objective you want to achieve.

It's your choice if you want to move on to work on any other objective or thought, or you can also just maintain that initial focus on the sound, object, or thought you first had.

Movement meditation

Movement meditation is another form of meditation you should try as well. This is a type of meditation where you focus on your breathing patterns, moving the air into and out of your lungs, while doing flowing movement patterns (with your hands) which you will repeat. You might feel uncomfortable at the beginning by moving with your eyes closed but with time you will notice it is actually very relaxing and will help you to improve your overall health.

A mind to body connection will be optimized in this type of meditation, especially for people who have trouble staying still and prefer to move around in a natural flowing motion. These movements should be slow and repetitive. The more controlled they are, the better. Doing fast, or violent movements will undo the benefit of meditating.

People who practice yoga often find this form of meditation great as it is a good compliment and similar to yoga breathing and movement exercises. Both improve control over yourself and over thoughts. For people who have never done yoga before and have already done movement meditation, will find that warming up with some yoga based exercises can often help you ease into movement meditation faster. The goal is to enter a meditative state quicker and yoga will definitely allow you to do this in a natural way. While yoga focuses more on improving flexibility and developing muscle strength, movement meditation is directed more towards a mental state and slow breathing patterns.

Mantra meditation

Mantra meditation is going to help you focus better on your thoughts and clear your mind to maximize the effect of meditating.

During mantra meditation you will be citing mantras over and over as you follow your meditative process.

A mantra could be a sound, phrase, or prayer that's chanted over and over.

We will not be focusing on spiritual meditation but it is another type of meditation besides focused meditation, mindfulness, mantra meditation, and movement meditation.

Everyone is different which means you don't have to use just one type of meditation to achieve your goals. You can use one or more forms of meditation and in different order.

CHAPTER 4: HOW TO PREPARE TO MEDITATE

Once you know what type of meditation you will be doing, you need to know how to prepare to meditate. Make sure not to rush through your meditation process as this will certainly reduce the overall effects and diminish possible results.

EQUIPMENT: Place a mat, blanket, towel, or chair where you plan to meditate.

Some people prefer to use a towel (which is great when you are traveling or out of town), or a mat to sit on or lay flat on your back on. Others prefer to sit on a chair to have a stable position that will help you not to fall asleep if you feel too relaxed.

I prefer to sit on a yoga mat as it is a position that I feel helps me focus and relax. Sometimes I warm up with yoga or static stretching so I will already have my mat ready but when I travel I simply use a thick towel.

Being comfortable is very important to get in the right state of mind so make sure you use the right equipment to get started.

TIME: Decide how long you will meditate for in advance

Make sure you decide beforehand for how long you plan on meditating and with what purpose. For something simple like focusing on being positive and breathing, you can plan on doing a short session of about 5 to 15 minutes long. Whereas if you plan on focusing on a problem and want to try and find a solution for, you might want to plan on giving yourself enough time to first relax through breathing patterns and then start to focus on alternative solutions to the problem at hand. This might take anywhere from 10 minutes to an hour or longer depending on your level of experience in meditating or it may also depend on how long it takes you to get in a relaxed state of mind that will allow you to focus well enough to confront the problem.

Plan on how long you will take so that you can prepare beforehand to stay at the same location until you're done without interruptions such as: being hungry, kids coming into the room, bathroom breaks, etc. Take care of these possible distractions beforehand.

LOCATION: Finding a clean, quiet, and comfortable space to meditate

Find a place where you can totally relax and clear your mind with no interruptions. This can be anywhere you feel comfortable and can reach this relaxed state of mind. It could be on the grass in a park, at home in your room, in your bathroom, in a quiet empty room, or by yourself in your car. This is completely up to you. Make sure you don't choose a location where you may have work close to you or a cell phone that keeps ringing or vibrating. TURN YOUR CELL PHONE OFF! It's impossible to get the results you want from meditating by having constant distractions and now a days cell phones are a main source of distraction and interruptions.

The location you choose should have these things in common: it should be quiet, clean, and needs to be at a cool room temperature (too warm will put you to sleep and too cold will make you want to get up and move around), it should be clear of distractions.

PREPARATION: Prepare your body to meditate

Before meditating make sure you do whatever you need to do to get your body relaxed and ready. This could be by taking a shower, stretching, putting on comfortable clothes, etc.

Make sure you eat at least 30 minutes before starting so that you don't feel hungry or too full. A lean meal would be ideal to help you prepare properly beforehand. I will go into more depth on the importance of nutrition in one of the following chapters.

WARM UP: Do some Yoga or stretch beforehand to start relaxing.

For some of you who have already done yoga in the past, know how relaxing it can be. Those of you who have not started doing yoga, it would be a good time to start since it will help you to better relax and calm yourself down. It's not necessary to do yoga before meditating but it helps in order to maximize the effects and speed up the relaxing process to get you in the right state of mind. Stretching is another good alternative since stretching combined with some breathing exercises will help you calm down and feel more at ease.

MENTALITY: Do some deep breathing to start calming yourself down

Breathing is easy but practicing breathing takes more time. The benefits of practicing breathing techniques are many.

Most athletes will find themselves recovering faster after intense moments. They will also notice they are able to stay focused even when out of breath. ATHLETES NEED TO LEARN TO BREATHE! Athletes need to focus on the air moving into and out of their lungs, pay attention to how the body expands and contracts. Hearing and feeling the air move in and out of your nose and mouth will help you feel more relaxed and is the proper to focus on your breathing. Every time you breathe in and is then exhaled try to focus on going into a deeper and deeper state of relaxation. Every time oxygen fills your lungs your body will feel more energized and full of positive emotions.

ENVIRONMENT: Add some meditative or relaxing music in the background only if it does not become a distraction.

If meditation music helps you get into a relaxed state, by all means include it in your meditation session. Everything and anything that helps you get into a more focused and relaxed state should be used, including music.

If you feel you are able to clear your mind better without any sounds or music, then don't add music to your environment.

I normally don't add music simply because I find music takes me in other directions which I don't always want to go since some music reminds me of other thoughts and ideas. That's just me but maybe music is right for you. Try both options to see what works better for you. Some athletes like to listen to music before competing since they feel it relaxes them or gets them in the right mood. Find what works for you and stick to it.

MEDITATING POSITIONS

When it comes to meditating positions it's basically up to you. There is no wrong or right position, only the one that gets you in the best state of concentration. For some people sitting on a chair is great because of the back support, while others prefer to be closer to the ground and will decide to sit on a towel.

For people who are less flexible the lotus position might be something you may want to skip or wait to try out as it might feel too uncomfortable to hold for a long period of time. Again, make sure you can stay in the same position for the time period you are planning to meditate for or else choose another position.

Sitting position

For the sitting position simply find a chair that you feel will allow you to focus without making you feel too uncomfortable or that relaxes you too much where you feel sleepy. Make sure your back is straight when seated and that your feet can touch the floor as you don't want to finish your meditation session with back pain. Some people prefer to add a soft pillow to their chair to feel more comfortable.

Kneeling on the floor

Take your shoes and socks off if you want to and kneel on the ground. Try kneeling on top of a soft mat or folded towel as to have your toes pointing behind you and your hips directly above your heels. Your back should be straight and relaxed as to allow your lungs to expand and contract as much times as necessary. You want to create a strong connection through your breathing and to do this, air has to go in and out of your lungs in a flowing motion.

Burmese position

The Burmese position is similar to a butterfly stretching position but with a change in the position of the feet. Sit down on the floor and open your legs, then bend your knees while bringing your feet towards the inside part of your legs. One foot should be in front of the other. When in this position try to keep your knees down as low as possible. If it feels uncomfortable choose another position as there are many options. Your hands should be at your sides or together in a finger crossing-over position. Your back should be straight and your forehead tilting slightly up and forward to allow you to take in air and release it in a full and complete manner. This is an advanced meditation position so it's not necessary to start with it unless you feel completely relaxed in it.

Lotus position

The Lotus position is very similar to the Burmese position but with a small alteration. You will need to bring your feet on top of your thighs while in a Burmese position. Your hands should be at your sides or together in a finger crossing-over position.

My knees feel uncomfortable in this position so I don't use it for my meditation sessions but you are free to try it as long as it does not cause pain. You don't want the pain you feel to take all your attention from your goal of focused breathing and calmness. If you don't like this position, simply choose another.

Laying down position

Lay down on the mat, towel, or blanket and relax your feet and hands. Your hands should stay at your sides and your feet pointing up or outwards. Your hands can be placed on your stomach in a gentle but still position or at your sides. Your head needs to stay facing the ceiling or the sky. If you tilt it to one side or another, this will not allow you to stay focused for long periods of time and might even end up with some neck tension. This is a great position to meditate in (when done correctly) as long as you don't fall asleep. If this is your problem, simply choose another position.

Butterfly position

In this position you will need to sit down on your mat or towel, open your legs and then bring your feet together so that the bottom of each is facing one another. Your knees might flare upwards or they might be able to go down to the ground, it does not matter as long as you feel comfortable and can relax in this position. Make sure your spine is straight and balanced.

CHAPTER 5: PERFORMANCE ENHANCING BREATHING PATTERNS ALL BODYBUILDERS SHOULD LEARN IN ORDER TO MEDITATE

Breathing patterns will be the key to set the pace of your meditation session and also to get into a hyper focused state.

For the mindfulness form of mediation you will continue to stay concentrated but you want to be more aware of your breathing. Your goal should not be to control your breathing but to simply feel the air going into your lungs and then out to your surroundings. The breathing in and out process should be done only through the nose for this specific type of meditation but should not be used for the other forms of meditation.

For the remainder of the other meditation types, you want to pay attention to breathing patterns and direct them through your session. All breathing patterns should be done by breathing in through your nose and out through your mouth (except when doing mindfulness meditation).

In order to get into a better meditative state, your heart rate needs to drop and to do this, breathing will be essential. The patterns you use will facilitate this process to help you reach higher levels of concentration. With practice these breathing patterns will become second nature to you. Decide beforehand if slow breathing patterns are better for you or if fast breathing patterns will be what you need. Slow breathing patterns relax you and fast breathing patterns energize you.

SLOW BREATHING PATTERNS

In order to slow down your breathing you will want to take in air slowly and for a longer period of time and then release it slowly as well. For athletes, this type of breathing is good to get you to relax after training or about an hour before competition. Different ratios of air in and air out will affect your level of relaxation, and in turn your ability to reach an optimal level of meditation.

Normal slow breathing pattern: Start by taking air in through your nose slowly and counting to 5. Then, release slowly counting back down from 5 to 1. You should repeat this process 4 to 10 times until you feel completely relaxed and ready to focus. Athletes should focus on breathing in through the nose and out through the mouth for this type of breathing pattern.

Extended slow breathing pattern: Start by taking air in through your nose slowly and counting to 7. Then, release slowly counting back down from 7 to 1 while exhaling out through your mouth. You should repeat this process 4 to 6 times until you feel completely relaxed and ready to focus.

Slow breathing pattern for hyperactive athletes: Start by taking air in through your nose slowly and counting to 3. Then, release slowly counting back down from 6 to 1 while exhaling out through your mouth. You should repeat this process 4 to 6 times until you feel relaxed and ready to focus. This pattern will force you to slow down completely. The last repetition of this sequence should end with 4 seconds in and 4 seconds out to stabilize your breathing.

Ultra slow breathing pattern: Begin by taking air in through your nose slowly and counting to 4. Then, release slowly counting back down from 10 to 1 while exhaling out through your mouth. You should repeat this process 4 to 6 times until you feel completely relaxed and ready to meditate. This pattern will force you to slow down gradually. The last 2 repetitions of this sequence should end with 4 seconds in and 4 seconds out to stabilize your breathing and balance the air in and out ratio.

Stabilizing breathing patterns before meditating: This is a good type of breathing pattern that should be used if you feel you are already calm and want to start immediately meditating. Start by taking air in through your nose slowly and counting to 3. Then, release slowly counting back down from 3 to 1. You should repeat this process 7 to 10 times until you feel completely relaxed and ready to focus. Athletes should focus on breathing in through the nose and out through the mouth for this type of breathing pattern.

FAST BREATHING PATTERNS

Fast breathing patterns are very important for athletes in order to get energized and ready to compete. Even though this type of breathing pattern is most effective when visualizing, it will be just as useful for meditating. For athletes that are very calm and need to feel more in control of their mind might want to use these patterns to get themselves ready to meditate.

Normal fast breathing pattern: Start by taking air in through your nose slowly and counting to 5. Then, release slowly counting back down from 3 to 1. You should repeat this process 6 to 10 times until you feel completely relaxed and ready to meditate. Athletes should focus on breathing in through the nose and out through the mouth for this type of breathing pattern.

Prolonged fast breathing pattern: Start by taking air in through your nose slowly and counting to 10. Then, release slowly counting back down from 5 to 1 while exhaling out through your mouth. You should repeat this process 5 to 6 times until you feel completely relaxed. If you have trouble getting to 10 at first, simply lower the count to 7 or 8. Focus on breathing in through the nose and out through the mouth.

Pre-competition fast breathing pattern: Start by taking air in through your nose slowly and counting to 6. Then, release quickly in one breath while exhaling out through your mouth. You should repeat this process 5 to 6 times until you feel completely relaxed and ready to focus. You can add 2 repetitions to this sequence with 4 seconds in and 4 seconds out to stabilize your breathing and balance the air in and out ratio.

All of these types of breathing patterns are performance enhancing and can be used during competition depending on your level of energy or nervousness.

For athletes that get nervous before competition you should use slow breathing patterns.

For athletes that need to get energized before competition you should use the fast breathing patterns.

In case of anxiety, a combination of slow breathing patterns followed by fast breathing patterns will give you optimal results.

During training sessions or during competition when feeling exhausted or out of breath use the normal fast breath breathing pattern to help recover quicker.

Breathing patterns are a great way to control your levels of intensity which in turn will save you energy and allow you to recover faster.

CHAPTER 6: DIET AND MEDITATION FOR BODYBUILDING

In order to get the best results from meditation, a good balanced diet will be necessary. Meditation is part of a collective goal to better yourself and proper nutrition will help you reach this goal. Eating right equates to having more energy and for extended periods of time. This in turn affects your capacity to stay focused for prolonged time periods. Lean proteins, omega fats, vegetables and legumes, and water are the best pre-meditation foods and should be eaten in appropriate amounts depending on your caloric needs.

Having too much sugar in your blood stream will force you to crash before, during, or after meditating and the same will happen in competition so refined sugars are not the way to go. Avoid large meals that might make you feel too full and will make you want to stop meditating or put you to sleep. Meals that are too small will make you hungry too soon which will shorten your meditation sessions and not allow you to maximize results.

Eating 60-75 minutes before meditating will give you more than sufficient time to digest and be ready to meditate properly.

Lean proteins

Lean proteins are very important to develop and repair muscle tissue. Lean proteins also help to normalize hormone concentrations in the body which will allow you to control your mood as well as your temper. Some of the best lean proteins you can have are:

- Turkey breast (all natural if possible).
- Lean red meat (all natural as well).
- Egg whites
- Most dairy products.
- Chicken breast (All natural).
- Quinoa
- Nuts (all varieties)

Omega fats

Omega fats are easy to obtain and very important for your body functions, especially for the brain. Omega fats are commonly found in:

- Salmon (Preferably wild, non-farmed)
- Walnuts (An easy to carry around snack)
- Flaxseeds (Blend them with any shake)
- Sardines

You will notice your brain functions improve and your brains' overall health increase. Your immune system should also get stronger which will reduce your chances of getting cancer, diabetes, and other serious health related problems.

Vegetables and Legumes

Vegetables and legumes are not given enough importance. Find a vegetable you enjoy eating and include it in your diet. It will pay off as the years go by. When you hear people talking about how important it is to have a balanced diet, they are also referring to vegetables. Some of the best vegetables and legumes to include in your daily meals are:

- Tomatoes
- Carrots
- Beets
- Kale
- Spinach
- Cabbage
- Parsley
- Broccoli
- Brussel sprouts
- Lettuce
- Radish
- Green, red, and yellow peppers
- Cucumber
- Egg plant
- Avocado

You want to make sure you get a wide variety of colors to make sure you get different vitamins and minerals.

Fruits

Fruits also contain a large amount of vitamins necessary for your body to perform to its maximum capacity. Antioxidants help your body to recover faster which is extremely important for athletes. Make sure you eat many fruits that are high on antioxidants after training or competing. Fruits provide an important source of dietary fiber which allows you to process food easier. Some of the best fruits to include in your pre-mediation diet are:

- Apples (green and red)
- Oranges
- Grapes (red and green)
- Bananas
- Grapefruit (A bit sour but full of antioxidants)
- Lemons and limes (In the form of juice mixed with water. I often ask for water and some slices of lemon when I go out to eat as these are wonderful antioxidants as well).
- Cherries (natural, not the sugar coated).
- Mandarins
- Watermelon
- Cantaloupe

Water

Water is commonly overlooked and most people don't drink enough of it. Fruit juices and milk should not be counted when considering how many glasses of water a day you take. Depending on the amount of cardiovascular training you do, this might be more than the usual suggested. Most people should drink at least 8 glasses of water a day but most athletes should drink 10 -14 glasses of water.

Ever since I started to carry around my gallon of water I am able to reach my "1 gallon a day" goal of water which has improved my health significantly.

Some of the benefits I have noticed and most people will notice are:

- Less or no headaches (Brain is hydrated more often)
- Improved digestion.
- Less tired during the day.
- More energy in the morning.
- Reduced amount of visible wrinkles.
- No cramps or signs of muscle tightness. (This is a common problem for many athletes.)
- Better concentration (this will benefit you a lot when meditating).
- Decreased desire for sweets and snacks in between meals.

SAMPLE MEAL RECIPES FOR PRE-MEDITATION SESSIONS

Here are some examples of lean meal recipes for athletes you can add to your pre-meditative diet. You can adapt them however you like in the size of the portions and ingredients used.

IF MEDITATING AFTER BREAKFAST

1. Quick start Breakfast

Snap your body out of a catabolic state and into a muscle-building one with this high-protein, high-carb oven-cooked breakfast. The grapefruit and asparagus make sure you get more than half a day's worth of vitamin C.

Ingredients (1serving):

6 egg whites

½ cup cooked quinoa and brown rice mix

3 asparagus spears, sliced

½ pink grapefruit

1 small red bell pepper, sliced

1 scoop flavorless whey protein powder

1 clove garlic, crushed

Olive oil spray

Pepper, salt

Prep time: 10 min

Cooking time: 15-20 min

Preparation:

Heat the oven to 200C fan/ gas 6. Lightly spray a cast iron skillet with olive oil.

In a medium bowl, whisk the egg whites with a pinch of salt and pepper until frothy.

Add the cooked brown rice and quinoa to the skillet; pour in the egg whites then the asparagus pieces and the bell pepper slices.

Bake in the oven for 15-20 min or until the eggs are cooked.

Nutritional value per serving: 407kcal, 52g protein, 40g carbs (5g fiber, 8g sugar), 2g fat, 15% calcium, 12% iron, 19% magnesium, 26% vitamin A, 63% vitamin C, 48% vitamin K, 12% vitamin B1, 69% vitamin B2, 26% vitamin B9.

2.   Complete Bowl

A breakfast with an appropriate name, the power bowl combines high in protein egg whites with energy fueling oatmeal. The walnuts add healthy fats and the honey tops everything with a bit of sweetness.

Ingredients (1 serving):

6 egg whites

½ cup instant oatmeal, cooked

1/8 cup walnuts

¼ cup berries

1 teaspoon raw honey

Cinnamon

Prep time: 10 min

Cooking time: 5 min

Preparation:

Whisk the egg whites until frothy then cook them in a skillet on low heat.

Combine the oatmeal and the egg whites in a bowl; add the cinnamon and raw honey and mix.

Top with berries, banana and walnuts.

Nutritional value per serving: 344kcal, 30g protein, 33g carbs (3g fiber, 23g sugar), 11g fat (2 saturated), 10% iron, 15% magnesium, 10% vitamin B1, 11% vitamin B2, 15% vitamin B5.

3. Tuna Stuffed Bell Peppers

This is a quick and nutritious recipe that provides a massive amount of B12. High in protein, tuna is an excellent breakfast option for muscle building and if you want to add some carbs to your meal, a piece of whole wheat toast is a great choice.

Ingredients (2 servings):

2 cans of tuna in water (185g), half drained

3 hard-boiled eggs

1 spring onion, finely chopped

5 small pickles, diced

salt, pepper

4 bell peppers, halved, with the seeds cleaned

Prep time: 5 min

Cooking time: 10 min

Preparation:

Combine the tuna, eggs, spring onion, pickles and seasoning in a food processor and mix until smooth.

Fill the halves of the bell peppers with the composition and serve.

Nutritional value per serving: 480kcal, 46g protein, 16g fat (4g saturated), 8g carbs (2g fiber, 4g sugar), 28%

magnesium, 94% vitamin A, 400% vitamin C, 12% vitamin E, 67% vitamin K, 18% vitamin B1, 32% vitamin B2, 90% vitamin B3, 20% vitamin B5, 56% vitamin B6, 18% vitamin B9, 284% vitamin B12.

4. Greek Yogurt with Flaxseeds and Apple

Branch out from the traditional egg white muscle-building breakfast and try some high-protein Greek Yogurt flavored with apple. Use whole flaxseeds to maximize your fiber intake and keep them in water overnight to get them soft and easily digestible.

Ingredients (1 serving):

1 cup Greek yogurt

1 apple, thinly sliced

2 tablespoons flaxseeds

¼ teaspoon cinnamon

1 teaspoon Stevia

A sprinkle of salt

Prep time: 5 min

Cooking time: 45 min

Preparation:

Preheat the oven to 190C fan/ gas 5. Place the apple slices in a non-stick pan, sprinkle them with cinnamon, Stevia and a dash of salt, cover them and bake for 45 min/ until tender. Remove them from the oven and allow them to cool for 30 min.

Place the Greek yogurt in a bowl then top with apples and flaxseeds and serve.

Nutritional value per serving: 422kcal, 22g protein, 39g carbs (7g fiber, 22 g sugar), 21g fat (8 g saturated), 14% calcium, 22% magnesium, 14% vitamin C, 24% vitamin B1, 13% vitamin B12.

5. Bell Pepper Rings with 'Fit Grits'

A tasty and special looking meal, the bell pepper rings with 'Fit Grits' fuel your muscles and give you enough energy to power through your day. Full of color and nutrients, this breakfast is high in vitamin B1.

Ingredients (1 serving):

6 egg whites

2 eggs

¼ cup brown rice farina

1 cup raw spinach

½ green bell pepper

1 cup of cherry tomatoes

olive oil spray

salt, pepper

Prep time: 10 min

Cooking time: 15 min

Preparation:

Whisk the egg whites with a pinch of salt and pepper until frothy. Heat some oil in a non-stick frying pan and cook the egg whites and farina. Add the spinach, mix together and cook until the spinach has wilted.

Lightly spray a skillet with olive oil and set on medium heat. Cut the bell peppers horizontally to create 2 rings, place them in the skillet and crack the eggs inside the bell peppers. Let them cook until the eggs turn white.

Place the egg-farina mixture and cooked pepper rings on a plate and serve with cherry tomatoes.

Nutritional value per serving : 495kcal, 45g protein, 45g carbs (3g fiber, 7g sugar), 11g fat (3g saturated), 9% calcium, 14% iron, 20% magnesium, 35% vitamin A, 32% vitamin C, 91% vitamin B2, 22% vitamin B5, 12% vitamin B6, 15% vitamin B12.

6. Almond Milk Smoothie

10 minutes is all you need to fix this high in vitamin D and B1 almond milk smoothie. You can fix a big batch and keep it in the freezer making this smoothie a perfect option for a quick breakfast to go.

Ingredients (2 serving):

1 cup almond milk

1 cup frozen mixed berries

1 cup spinach

1 scoop banana flavored protein powder

1 tablespoon chia seeds

Prep time: 10 min

No cooking

Preparation:

Mix all the ingredients in a blender until smooth, pour into 2 glasses and serve.

Nutritional value per serving: 295kcal, 26g protein, 32g carbs (4g fiber, 13g sugar), 9g fat, 40% calcium, 20% iron,

12% magnesium, 50% vitamin A, 40% vitamin C, 25% vitamin D, 57% vitamin E, 213% vitamin B1, 18% vitamin B9.

7.   Pumpkin Pie Protein Pancakes

Forget about flour and try oat pancakes with a delicious addition of fresh pumpkin. Topple some calorie-free syrup and enjoy a high-protein breakfast that tastes as good as a cheat meal.

Ingredients (1 serving):

1/3 cup old-fashioned oats

¼ cup pumpkin

½ cup egg whites

1 scoop cinnamon protein powder

½ teaspoon cinnamon

Olive oil spray

Prep time: 5 min

Cooking time: 5 min

Preparation:

Mix all the ingredients together in a bowl. Spray a medium-sized skillet with olive oil then place on medium heat.

Pour in the batter, and once you see tiny bubbles appear on the top of the pancake, flip. When each side is golden, remove the pancake and serve.

Nutritional value per serving: 335kcal, 39g protein, 37g carbs (6g fiber, 1 g sugar), 6g fat, 14% calcium, 15% iron, 26% magnesium, 60% vitamin A, 26% vitamin B1, 37% vitamin B2, 10% vitamin B5, 31% vitamin B6.

8. High-protein Oatmeal

Lasso in a hearty helping of carbs that will keep you satiated for hours, while the protein powder and almonds will deliver a protein-packed start to your day. If you prefer you oatmeal with a fruity taste, use banana flavored protein powder.

Ingredients (1 serving):

2 packets of instant oatmeal (28g packet)

¼ cup ground almonds

1 scoop of vanilla flavored whey protein powder

1 tablespoon cinnamon

Prep time: 5 min

Cooking time: 5 min

Preparation:

Pour the instant oatmeal into a bowl, mix with the protein powder and cinnamon. Add hot water and mix. Top with crushed almonds and serve.

Nutritional value per serving: 436kcal, 33g protein, 45g carbs (10g fiber, 4g sugar), 15g fat (1g saturated), 17% calcium, 19% iron, 37% magnesium, 44% vitamin E, 21% vitamin B1, 21% vitamin B2.

9. Protein-packed Scramble

Feed your muscles and push through an intense workout with this 51g protein meal. These scrambled egg whites with vegetables and turkey sausage have the added value of being packed with carbs and overall high amounts of vitamins.

Ingredients (1 serving):

8 egg whites

2 link turkey sausages, chopped

1 large onion, diced

1 cup red bell peppers, diced

2 tomatoes, diced

2 cups raw spinach, chopped

1 teaspoon olive oil

Salt and pepper

Prep time: 10 min

Cooking time: 10-15 min

Preparation:

Whisk the egg whites with a pinch of salt and pepper until frothy, then set aside.

Heat the oil in a large non-stick pan, drizzle the onions and peppers and sauté until they are tender. Season with salt and pepper. Add the turkey sausage and cook until it is golden brown then lower the heat and add the egg whites and scramble.

When the eggs are almost done, add the tomato and spinach, cook for 2 min and serve.

Nutritional value per serving: 475kcal, 51g protein, 37g carbs (10g fiber, 18g sugar), 10g fat (2g saturated), 14% calcium, 23% iron, 37% magnesium, 255% vitamin A, 516% vitamin C, 25% vitamin E, 397% vitamin K, 22% vitamin B1, 112% vitamin B2, 29% vitamin B3, 19% vitamin B5, 51% vitamin B6, 65% vitamin B9.

10. Fruit and Peanut Butter Smoothie

What better way to get your day's worth of calcium than with this strawberry flavored smoothie? High in minerals, vitamins, protein and energy fueling carbs, this smoothie is a perfect way to kick-start your day.

Ingredients (1 serving):

15 medium-sized strawberries

1 1/3 tablespoons peanut butter

85g tofu

½ cup fat free yogurt

¾ cup skim milk

1 scoop protein powder

8 ice cubes

Prep time: 5min

No cooking

Preparation:

Pour the milk into the blender then the yogurt and the rest of the ingredients. Blend until mixture is completely blended and frothy. Pour into a glass and serve.

Nutritional value per serving: 472kcal, 45g protein, 40g carbs (6g fiber, 31g sugar), 13g fat (4g saturated), 110% calcium, 35% iron, 27% magnesium, 30% vitamin A, 190% vitamin C, 11% vitamin E, 13% vitamin B1, 24% vitamin B2, 10% vitamin B5, 18% vitamin B6, 17% vitamin B9, 12% vitamin B12.

11. Whey Protein Muffins

With a healthy dose of oats and a serving of chocolate whey protein powder, these muffins are a great breakfast alternative to regular oats. Paired with a glass of milk, this meal makes sure that you get a good amount of calcium and vitamin D to go with the nice protein and carbs serving.

Ingredients (4 muffins-2 servings):

1 cup rolled oats

1 large whole egg

5 large egg whites

½ scoop chocolate whey protein powder

Olive oil spray

2 cups of low fat milk, to serve

Prep time: 2 min

Cooking time: 15 min

Preparation:

Preheat the oven to 190C fan/ gas 5.

Blend all the ingredients together for 30s. Spray the muffin tin with olive oil then batter up into four muffins. Place in the oven for 15 min.

Remove from the oven, let them cool and serve with the glass of milk.

Nutritional value per serving (includes milk): 330kcal, 28g protein, 37g carbs (9g fiber, 13g sugar), 6g fat (5g saturated), 37% calcium, 22% iron, 19% magnesium, 12% vitamin A, 34% vitamin D, 44% vitamin B1, 66% vitamin B2, 25% vitamin B5, 11% vitamin B6, 24% vitamin B12.

12. Smoked Salmon and Avocado with Toast

Are you in for a tough workout and low on time? It only takes 5 min to piece together this savory breakfast. Both the salmon and avocado are high in healthy acids and this meal has enough protein and carbs to keep you motivated.

Ingredients (2 servings):

300g smoked salmon

2 medium-sized ripe avocados, stoned and peeled

Juice from ½ lemon

A handful tarragon leaves, chopped

2 slices of whole wheat bread, toasted

Prep time: 5 min

No cooking time

Preparation:

Cut the avocados into chunks and toss in the lemon juice. Twist and fold the smoked salmon pieces, place them on serving plates, then scatter with the avocado and tarragon. Serve with whole wheat toast.

Nutritional value per serving: 550kcal, 34g protein, 37g carbs (12g fiber, 4g sugar), 30g fat (5g saturated), 17% iron, 24% magnesium, 25% vitamin C, 27% vitamin E, 42% vitamin K, 16% vitamin B1, 24% vitamin B2, 55% vitamin B3, 35% vitamin B5, 40% vitamin B6, 35% vitamin B9, 81% vitamin B12.

13. Low-carb 'Pizza'

Forget about the high-calorie, non-nutritious slice of pizza and replace it with this delicious substitute. Healthy and filling, it only takes 20 min to make and it's not only high in protein, but also in minerals and vitamins.

Ingredients (1 serving):

1 small whole wheat pita

3 egg whites

1 egg

¼ cup low-fat mozzarella cheese

1 spring onion, sliced

¼ cup mushrooms, diced

¼ cup bell peppers, diced

2 slices turkey bacon, chopped

1 teaspoon olive oil

Salt and pepper

Prep time: 10 min

Cooking time: 10 min

Preparation:

Whisk the eggs with a pinch of salt and pepper and add the diced vegetables.

Bend the edges of the pita bread to create a bowl. Brush both sides with the olive oil and place the pita bread on the grill, dome side down. Cook until golden then flip it on the other side.

Pour the egg mix into the pita and cook until the eggs are nearly done, add the turkey bacon, spring onion and cheese. Cook until the cheese had melted and serve.

Nutritional value per serving: 350kcal, 33g protein, 12g carbs (3g fiber, 4g sugar), 15g fat (6 saturated), 32% calcium, 19% iron, 15% magnesium, 36% vitamin A, 88% vitamin C, 72% vitamin K, 21% vitamin B1, 71% vitamin B2, 22% vitamin B3, 14% vitamin B5, 21% vitamin B6, 25% vitamin B9, 29% vitamin B12.

14. Mexican Mocha Breakfast

Top your favorite cup of oats with a healthy serving of almond milk and enjoy a quickly-made high-fiber breakfast. The cayenne pepper is perfect for adding a little oomph to your oatmeal.

Ingredients (1 serving):

½ cup rolled oats

1 scoop chocolate protein powder

½ tablespoon cinnamon

½ teaspoon cayenne pepper

1 cup unsweetened almond milk

1 tablespoon unsweetened cocoa powder

Prep time: 5 min

Cooking time: 3 min

Preparation:

Mix all the ingredients in a microwave-safe bowl. Heat in the microwave for 2 ½ -3 min then serve.

Nutritional value per serving: 304kcal, 27g protein, 38g carbs (8g fiber, 3g sugar), 7g fat, 32% calcium, 15% iron, 25% magnesium, 10% vitamin A, 25% vitamin D, 51% vitamin E, 12% vitamin B1.

15. Blueberry Lemon Pancakes (any time)

A warm, filling breakfast, this blueberry pancake enriched by the lemony flavor is a simple and tasty way of getting that high-powered meal that you need to start your day. Spread a tablespoon of Greek yogurt on top of your pancake if you like.

Ingredients (1 serving):

1/3 cup oat bran

5 egg whites

½ cup blueberries

1 scoop flavorless whey protein powder

½ teaspoon baking soda

1 teaspoon grated lemon peel

1 tablespoon lemon drink mix

olive oil spray

Prep time: 5 min

Cooking time: 5 min

Preparation:

Combine all the ingredients in a large bowl, mix and whisk until smooth.

Cook the batch in a sprayed skilled on medium-high temperature until bubbles form on the surface. Flip over and cook until each side is dark golden brown. Remove the pancake and serve.

Nutritional value per serving: 340kcal, 47g protein, 37g carbs (6g fiber, 14g sugar), 5g fat, 10% iron, 25% magnesium, 12% vitamin C, 19% vitamin K, 26% vitamin B1, 58% vitamin B2.

PRE-MEDITATION LUNCH

16.   Mediterranean Rice

Turn the tired can of tuna into a delicious dish that is a perfect starter for an afternoon of exercise. The high amount of carbs will fuel a thorough workout and the protein will make sure that your muscles recuperate from the effort.

Ingredients (1 serving):

1 can of tuna in oil, drained

100g brown rice

¼ avocado, chopped

¼ red onion, sliced

Juice from ½ lemon

Salt and pepper

Prep time: 5 min

Cooking time: 20 min

Preparation:

Boil the brown rice for approximately 20 min then place in a bowl with the onion, tuna and avocado. Add the lemon juice and mix all the ingredients. Season with salt and pepper to taste and serve.

Nutritional value per serving: 590kcal, 32g protein, 80g carbs (7g fiber, 1g sugar), 14g fat (5g saturated), 22% iron, 52% magnesium, 101% vitamin D, 18% vitamin E, 107% vitamin K, 32% vitamin B1, 134% vitamin B3, 26% vitamin B5, 39% vitamin B6, 15% vitamin B9, 63% vitamin B12.

17. Spiced Chicken

Chicken is perfect for a high protein muscle building meal. High in nutrients across the board, this simple, tasty meal can be paired with a serving of your choice of carbs.

Ingredients (2 servings):

3 boneless chicken breasts cut in half

175g low-fat yogurt

5cm piece cucumber, finely chopped

2 tablespoons Thai red curry paste

2 tablespoons cilantro, chopped

2 cups raw spinach, to serve.

Prep time: 5 min

Cooking time: 35-40 min

Preparation:

Preheat the oven to 190C fan/ gas 5. Put the chicken in a dish in one layer. Blend a third of the yogurt, the curry paste and two thirds of the cilantro, add salt and pour over the chicken, making sure the meat is evenly coated. Leave for 30 min (or in the fridge overnight).

Lift the chicken onto a rack in a roasting tin for 35-40 min, until golden.

Heat water in a pan and wilt the spinach.

Mix the rest of the yogurt and cilantro, add the cucumber and stir. Pour the mix over the chicken and serve with the cooked spinach.

Nutritional value per serving: 275kcal, 43g protein, 8g carbs (1g fiber, 8g sugar), 3g fat (1g saturated), 20% calcium, 15% iron, 25% magnesium, 56% vitamin A, 18% vitamin C, 181% vitamin K, 16% vitamin B1, 26% vitamin B2, 133% vitamin B3, 25% vitamin B5, 67% vitamin B6, 19% vitamin B9, 22% vitamin B12.

18. Stuffed Eggs with Pita Bread

Get your fill of omega-3 fatty acids with this rich salmon dish. High in vitamins and minerals, this filling meal is a great way of boosting yourself with energy and powering through your day.

Ingredients (2 servings):

1 canned salmon in water (450g)

2 eggs

1 large spring onions, finely chopped

2 large leafs of lettuce

10 cherry tomatoes

1 tablespoon Greek yogurt

A large whole wheat pita bread, cut in half

Sea salt and pepper

Prep time: 10 min

Cooking time: 10 min

Preparation:

Boil the eggs, peel them and slice them in half then remove the yolks and place them in a bowl.

Add the canned salmon, 1 tablespoon of yogurt, the spring onion and the seasonings to the bowl. Mix all the ingredients together and stuff the egg whites. Serve with pita bread stuffed with lettuce and tomatoes.

Nutritional value per serving: 455kcal, 45g protein, 24g carbs (3g fiber, 2g sugar), 36g fat (10g saturated), 59% calcium, 22% iron, 21% magnesium, 30% vitamin A, 24% vitamin C, 43% vitamin K, 11% vitamin B1, 36% vitamin B2, 60% vitamin B3, 20% vitamin B5, 41% vitamin B6, 20% vitamin B9, 20% vitamin B12.

19. Chicken Caesar Wraps

These chicken wraps make a great portable meal that will make sure that you keep your protein levels high throughout the day. Throw in some baby spinach and make a more green friendly meal.

Ingredients (1 serving):

85g chicken breast, baked

2 whole wheat tortillas

1 cup lettuce

50g non-fat yogurt

1 teaspoon anchovy paste

1 teaspoon dry mustard powder

1 clove garlic, cooked

½ medium cucumber, chopped

Prep time: 5 min

No cooking

Preparation:

Combine the anchovy paste, garlic and yogurt then toss and coat the lettuce and cucumbers. Split the mix in 2, add to the tortillas and then place half the chicken in each tortilla. Wrap up and serve.

Nutritional value per serving (2 tortillas): 460kcal, 41g protein, 57g carbs (7g fiber, 9g sugar), 10g fat (2g saturated), 11% calcium, 22% vitamin K, 13% vitamin B2, 59% vitamin B3, 12% vitamin B5, 29% vitamin B6, 10% vitamin B12.

PRE-MEDITATION DINNER

20. Baked Salmon with Grilled Asparagus

A classic dish, made more interesting by a marinade of lemon juice and mustard, this grilled salmon goes well with the garlicky asparagus spears. Treat yourself to a great combination of protein and vitamins.

Ingredients (1 serving):

140g wild salmon

1 ½ cup asparagus

Marinade:

1 tablespoon garlic, minced

1 tablespoon Dijon mustard

Lemon juice from ½ lemon

1 teaspoon olive oil

Prep time: 5 min

Cooking time: 15 min

Preparation:

Preheat oven to 200C fan/ gas 6.

In a bowl, mix the lemon juice, half the garlic, olive oil and mustard, pour the marinade over the salmon and make sure it is completely covered. Place the marinating salmon in the fridge for at least one hour.

Cut the bottom stems off the asparagus spears. Set a nonstick skillet on medium/high heat, toss the asparagus with the remaining garlic and sear for about 5 min, rolling the asparagus on all sides.

Place the salmon on a baking sheet and bake for 10 min then serve with the grilled asparagus.

Nutritional value: 350kcal, 43g protein, 7g carbs (5g fiber, 1 g sugar), 16g fat (1 saturated), 17% iron, 20% magnesium, 48% vitamin A, 119% vitamin C, 17% vitamin E, 288% vitamin K, 39% vitamin B1, 60% vitamin B2, 90% vitamin B3, 33% vitamin B5, 74% vitamin B6, 109% vitamin B9, 75% vitamin B12.

21. Beef Meatball Pasta with Spinach

A high-protein pasta meal that makes the most of the beef and spinach pairing. Not only is it all-round vitamin packed, but it also contains a hearty amount of magnesium which helps regulate muscle contraction.

Ingredients (2 servings):

For meatballs:

170g lean ground beef

½ cup raw spinach, shredded

1 tablespoon minced garlic

¼ cup red onion, diced

1 teaspoon cumin

Sea salt and pepper

For Pasta:

100g wheat spinach pasta

10 cherry tomatoes

2 cups raw spinach

¼ cup marinara

2 tablespoons low-fat parmesan cheese

Prep time: 15 min

Cooking time: 30 min

Preparation:

Preheat oven to 200C/ gas 6.

Mix together the ground beef, raw spinach, garlic, red onion and salt and pepper to taste. Mix thoroughly with your hands until the spinach is completely mixed into the meat.

Form two or three meatballs, roughly the same size then place them on a baking sheet in the oven for 10-12 minutes.

Cook the pasta according to the instructions on the pack. Drain the pasta and stir in the tomatoes, spinach and cheese. Add the meatballs and serve.

Nutritional value per serving: 470kcal, 33g protein, 50g carbs (6g fiber, 5g sugar), 12g fat (5g saturated), 17% calcium, 28% iron, 74% magnesium, 104% vitamin A, 38% vitamin C, 11% vitamin E, 361% vitamin K, 16% vitamin B1,

20% vitamin B2, 45% vitamin B3, 11% vitamin B5, 45% vitamin B6, 35% vitamin B9, 37% vitamin B12.

22. Stuffed Chicken Breast with Brown Rice

Brown rice is an excellent way of introducing quality carbs to your diet. Couple it with high-protein chicken breast and some vegetables and you have a delicious power lunch.

Ingredients (1 serving):

170g chicken breast

½ cup raw spinach

50g brown rice

1 spring onion, diced

1 tomato, sliced

1 tablespoon feta cheese

Prep time: 10 min

Cooking time: 30 min

Preparation:

Preheat the oven to 190C fan/ gas 5.

Slice the chicken breast down the middle to make it look like a butterfly. Season the chicken with salt and pepper, then open it and layer spinach, feta cheese and tomato slices on one side. Fold the chicken breast and use a toothpick to hold it closed then bake for 20 min.

Boil the brown rice then add the garlic and chopped onion. Fill a plate with brown rice, place the chicken on top and serve.

Nutritional value per serving: 469kcal, 48g protein, 46g carbs (5g fiber, 6g sugar), 8g fat (5g saturated), 22% calcium, 18% iron, 38% magnesium, 55% vitamin A, 43% vitamin C, 169% vitamin K, 28% vitamin B1, 28% vitamin B2, 103% vitamin B3, 28% vitamin B5, 70% vitamin B6, 23% vitamin B9, 17% vitamin B12.

23.   Shrimp and Zucchini Linguine Pasta Salad

A cheat pasta meal with a serving of shredded zucchini and steamed shrimp flavored with all manners of sesame. This combination of ingredients makes for a light lunch with a high-protein content.

Ingredients (1 serving):

170g steamed shrimp

1 large zucchini, chopped

¼ cup red onion, sliced

1 cup bell peppers, sliced

1 tablespoon roasted Tahini butter

1 teaspoon sesame oil

1 teaspoon sesame seeds

Prep time: 10 min

No cooking

Preparation:

Cut the zucchini using a shredder in order to make raw linguine.

In a bowl, mix tahini and sesame oil.

Place all the ingredients in a large bowl, pour the Tahini sauce and toss it to make sure all sides are covered in sauce. Sprinkle some sesame seeds and serve.

Nutritional value per serving: 420kcal, 45g protein, 26g carbs (10g fiber, 12g sugar), 18g fat (2g saturated), 19% calcium, 47% iron, 48% magnesium, 33% vitamin A, 303% vitamin C, 17% vitamin E, 31% vitamin K, 38% vitamin B1, 36% vitamin B2, 38% vitamin B3, 13% vitamin B5, 66% vitamin B6, 35% vitamin B9, 42% vitamin B12.

24. Turkey Meatloaf with Whole Wheat Couscous

Cooked in a muffin pan, this turkey meatloaf makes sure that you minimize you saturated fats intake. Mix it up a little by adding bell pepper or mushrooms instead of onion into the meatballs and by seasoning with a pinch of ground garlic.

Ingredients (1 serving):

140g lean ground turkey

¾ cup red onions, diced

1 cup raw spinach

1/3 cup low sodium marinara sauce

½ cup whole wheat couscous, boiled

Choice of seasoning: Parsley, Basil, Coriander

Pepper, salt

Olive oil spray

Prep time: 5 min

Cooking time: 20 min

Preparation:

Preheat oven to 200C fan/ gas 6.

Season turkey with your choice of seasoning and add the diced onions.

Light spray your muffin pan with olive oil, place the ground turkey inside the muffin holders. Top each turkey meatball with 1 tablespoon marinara sauce, then place in the oven and bake for 8-10 min.

Serve with couscous.

Nutritional value per serving: 460kcal, 34g protein, 53g carbs (4g fiber, 7g sugar), 12g fat (4g saturated), 12% calcium, 15% iron, 10% magnesium, 16% vitamin A, 15% vitamin C, 11% vitamin E, 16% vitamin K, 11% vitamin B1, 25% vitamin B3, 16% vitamin B6, 11% vitamin B9.

CHAPTER 7: THE POWER OF USING VISUALIZATIONS FOR BODYBUILDING

What does it mean to visualize?

Visualizing is basically to conceptualize an image of something in your mind that you want to achieve and want to find a path towards that objective. You are fundamentally doing everything you want to do when you perform but it is done through your imagination and in your mind. As you have often heard "If you can see it, you can do it".

There is no wrong or right way of visualizing. You are going to find a comfortable place. Either sit or rest on a comfortable chair, mat, or towel much like you do when you meditate.

When you visualize you are taking meditation to the next level and want to use much of the same process you do for meditating.

There are many types of visualizations that can be done. Three common ones are motivational visualizations, problem solving visualizations, and goal oriented visualizations.

Athletes in all fields commonly use visualizations in one form or another sometimes without even knowing they are doing them. For some, it's done while awake which is what is known as visualizations and for others this might happen in their dreams but with no control over the outcome.

When you visualize you are envisioning images or mental videos of what you would like to see which could include:

- How you look.
- How you're dressed.
- How you move.
- How you perform.
- What emotional state you are in.
- What mental state you're in.
- What the results of your competition are.

You are in control of everything you're seeing in your mind and can design the beginning and ending however you like. Being creative is useful since things don't always come out the way we plan them to in real life but by preparing mentally and emotionally for possible situations and results, things become easier to handle when it comes time to perform. Peak performance is a term used for when you are "in the zone" and at your very best. It is easier to perform at your peak when you have prepared your mind through visualizations.

Why visualize to motivate yourself?

Some people have trouble finding the right motivation under pressure to do what they are supposed to do instead of being intimidated by their surroundings and people watching them. By motivating yourself through visualizations and by telling yourself to do better and push yourself harder as you see the thoughts you want to realize in your mind, you will unlock the brains possibilities to get you through the fear, anxiety, nervousness, and pressure involved when competing.

What are goal oriented visualizations

Goal oriented visualizations are mental images and videos you want to create in your brain when visualizing that focus on achieving a specific objective. This may be: winning a competition, improving your time, training more hours a day, adding more protein to your diet, not getting tired as much (some of these are results based goals and some are performance based goals. Both are important when planning your visualization session.)

This is what you train physically for. To see results at the end of all the hard work. Using visualizations completes the training by doing the last and most important part of preparing for competition. You have to prepare your mind and body to perform at their best. Nutrition and physical training will prepare your body. Meditation, breathing patterns, and visualizations will train your brain. The combination of both will give you the greatest competitive advantage and that's you want.

CHAPTER 8: MEDITATING FOR MAXIMUM BODYBUILDING RESULTS

Meditating to reach your maximum potential will depend on your ability to focus on a thought or problem and stay focused for as long as necessary to solve the problem or until you realize your objective. This will create confidence and self-conviction for future tasks you may need to accomplish.

When you meditate and want to achieve maximum results you will need to follow these exact steps every time. If you change or eliminate any step, you will end up changing the outcome of the meditation session.

These steps are:

1st: Find a quiet place where you won't be disturbed.

2nd: Place a mat, towel, blanket, or chair where you are planning to meditate.

3rd: Make sure you had a light meal or snack about an hour before meditating.

4th: Choose a position in which you will be comfortable in for the entire session. This could be: sitting on a chair, lying down on a mat, sitting in a Burmese, Lotus or butterfly position, kneeling on a mat, or any other comfortable meditation position mentioned before.

5th: Begin your breathing pattern. If you want to calm and relax yourself you should choose to breathe more air out than you do air in (except if you are doing mindfulness meditation as you should not try to control your breathing but instead simply feel the air going into your lungs and then out into your surroundings.). For example, breathe in 4 seconds and then breathe out for 6 seconds. When trying to energize yourself because you feel too relaxed or just woke up, you would breathe more air in than out in a specific ratio which you can decide beforehand. For example, breathe 5 seconds in and 3 seconds out. Remember each sequence of breathing needs to be repeated at least 4 to 6 times to allow your breathing to slow the mind down and get you in a state of calmness to best meditate. For all breathing patterns you will breathe in through your nose and out through your mouth, except for mindfulness meditation which will be in and out through your nose only as the focus is not on your breathing.

6th: Once you are done completing your breathing patterns in the manner explained in the breathing patterns chapter, you should begin to focus on something you want to obtain, achieve, or simply preview in your mind. Focus on this for as long as possible. Short sessions give you shorter lasting results while longer sessions tend to help you maintain this level of concentration even after you're done meditating. All athletes know that when it's time to perform, (especially when under pressure), they need to stay focused and being able to do this for a longer period of time without losing concentration will permit them to outperform the competition. **This is the difference between champions and the rest!**

7th: This thought should now evolve to a short or long mental movie clip you are creating in your mind to help you achieve what you want in your mind first, with the goal to eventually make it happen in a real life situation. Be as specific as possible and stay relaxed in the process. This seventh step adds visualizing to the process but there's nothing wrong with that as it can only benefit you but it's necessary if you just want to keep it simple.

8th: Athletes need to use breathing to finish their meditation sessions to end as they began. If you don't have to compete on the same day, you can use slow breathing patterns such as the example below:

Normal slow breathing pattern: Start by taking air in through your nose slowly and counting to 5. Then, release slowly counting back down from 5 to 1. You should repeat this process 4 to 10 times until you feel completely relaxed and ready to meditate. Athletes should focus on breathing in through the nose and out through the mouth for this type of breathing pattern.

If you have to compete the same day you should energize your mind and body at the end by using fast breathing patterns such as the one below:

Normal fast breathing pattern: Start by taking air in through your nose slowly and counting to 5. Then, release slowly counting back down from 3 to 1. You should repeat this process 6 to 10 times until you feel completely relaxed but energized. Athletes should focus on breathing in through the nose and out through the mouth for this type of breathing pattern.

For athletes who are doing mindfulness meditation, their sessions should end once they are done meditating as the focus behind this form of meditation is not breathing but instead to calm the mind and focus on a specific thought.

IT ONLY WORKS IF YOU BELIEVE IT WILL WORK SO BE PATIENT AND BE PERSISTENT!

CHAPTER 9: MEDITATING FOR EMOTIONAL STRENGTH

The emotional strain behind every competition is overwhelming, tiring, and exhausting. Preparing yourself to overcome emotional stress is very important and necessary to overcome mental hurdles.

Some athletes are great when training but fall apart under emotional stress when competing, but meditating can improve your approach to this kind of stress. Some will yell, scream, complain, lower their heads, show low self-esteem, appear with low energy, cry, or even be nervous. This is normal under pressure situations but it can be a problem easily fixed through meditation. Let's look at some problems and solutions that you can focus on when meditating.

Why do I feel insecure when I am competing?

Insecurity can happen for a number of reasons. For some, its lack of preparation where you might feel you're not prepared to compete. For this problem simply prepare as much as you need to until you feel ready. Don't get pressured into competing if you're not ready.

For others, insecurity might come from comparing yourself too much with others instead of focusing on your results and improving off past results. Focus on seeing yourself improve through training and better preparation when you meditate.

Why do I get angry with myself and others when I am competing?

Anger is a common reaction for many athletes when they are under pressure and don't know what to do. Other times anger can be a result of frustration. Some people get angry with themselves, others with the competition, many with people close to them, and lastly at external conditions they have no control over.

When meditating, you can overcome this problem by trying to focus on accepting that there are things you have no control over and can only anticipate them and have an alternate plan if they occur. Accept weather conditions, noise, or delays which are possible situations which can happen but can have different consequences on you depending on your level of preparation.

There will also be circumstances in which you will have control over situations and can prevent getting angry.

If there is someone you prefer not having around when you compete, simply ask them politely to wait for you to finish and then can share the triumph with you later. They should understand if they truly desire the best for you and that's the way it should be.

When you feel angry because you're not competing the way you believe you could, meditation would definitely help you to plan things better by using your meditating time to prepare a path or a step by step process to follow that will give you the best possible chance to perform at your true potential.

Why am I so afraid during a competition?

Fear is one of the most common conditions all athletes suffer from. It's a human emotion in reaction to a threat. Fear comes in different forms and sizes. Some types of fear are based on events or things that don't really exist but are created in your mind. These are often things that could happen but might never happen at all. Let me repeat the last part "could happen but might never happen at all".

Fear of future outcomes are a waste of energy and will drain you emotionally. Future outcomes are a result of present planning and proper preparation. If you focus on results based goals and achieve them during competition, most of the time you will obtain your results based goals.

For example, focusing on being positive and adaptive no matter what the situation, will help you overcome difficult conditions and many times have a positive result at the end mainly because you did not stop believing in yourself and didn't give up.

Fear can also be due to a current threat that is small in nature but because you think so much on it you end up building it up to a huge problem and a huge fear. Never let this happen because you will make it impossible for your mind to overcome a situation like this. If your climbing a hill, don't look at it like Mount Everest because you'll want to quit before you even start.

Give each circumstance and problem the attention it deserves and no more. Meditate on focusing on one thing and once you are done with it focus on something else. You don't have to over analyze hundreds of outcomes when there might be a less than a 1% chance they might even happen.

When you meditate you try to see yourself in a different image. Use your mind to see yourself as you wish. For example, you could choose to see yourself as a confident, fearless, and aggressive person.

Don't give others more credit than their due and don't cut yourself short. Being overconfident is better than being fearful and being sure of yourself is better than being overconfident. Find the right balance and build that image in your mind then try to live that image on a daily basis.

I feel so nervous when I'm under pressure, why is this?

Being nervous can actually be a good thing as it can have a positive affect over your mind and body. How can nerves be good you ask? For some people, being nervous can bring out the best in themselves and compete better than they usually would. In other circumstances, your body might trigger adrenaline to naturally enhance your senses and physical capabilities.

Being nervous might also cause the opposite affect and make you freeze when you need to react. This is a huge and very obvious problem.

When meditating you often improve your breathing pattern skills and learn to control the flow of air in your body. This is a very useful skill that has a powerful effect on nervousness and your emotions in general.

Becoming Mentally Tougher In Bodybuilding by Using Meditation

Three things you can do when you're under pressure are:

1. Take deep breaths and slow your heart rate down. (Meditation will greatly improve this practice and better prepare you for when you're nervous).
2. Staying active (the opposite reaction would be to stay still or to "freeze" which is bad. Stay active doing whatever you need to be doing to help keep your cool. Some people chew gum or sun flower seeds, others move their feet, and some listen to music, while others try to distract themselves before competing by reading books or talking to others. There are many more ways of staying active but you have to choose one that's right for you.)
3. Thinking positive thoughts (Meditation is often used to slow the mind and relax the body which then allows your brain to concentrate on productive thoughts which should be positive. Use meditation to help you become more positive by practicing positive thinking in your sessions.)

CHAPTER 10: MEDITATING FOR MENTAL TOUGHNESS

What is mental toughness?

Being mentally tough can mean many things but for athletes it means not falling under pressure and meeting any challenge head on with the power of the mind.

Is mental toughness important?

Yes, it's very important. As you become more and more advanced you will notice that your body can only take you so far and the mind is the one that has to take control over the future of your results. Being mentally tough will permit you to take control of these future results and push you to your limit thanks to the efforts made when meditating for mental toughness.

How can I use mental toughness in bodybuilding?

In bodybuilding, mental toughness is a skill that needs to be developed over time but that will be reliable when it's time to perform. Mental toughness can be used in many ways. It can be used to stay calm under pressure. It can also be used to enhance your performance. Lastly, it can be used to outlast the competition when you feel your body is can go no further.

Three examples of mental toughness skills that you could develop for bodybuilding when meditating for mental toughness would be:

1. **Using proper mental vocabulary.** Most of us have inner conversations with ourselves and the words we use have a huge impact on our actions. Telling your body "not to give up" is an example of having a negative mental vocabulary. If you tell your body to "keep going", you would be using a positive mental vocabulary. With the first, your brain searches for key words and in this case it hears the words "give up" even though you are trying to force it to hear "not to give up". This is simply how the brain works. In the second example, the brain hears the key words "keep going" and continues going. Shorter isn't the solution, simply the key words you use. Stay away from using any words that could allow the brain to associate actions you don't want happening.
2. **Projecting a confident image of yourself.** By forcing yourself to stand straight, your hands to relax, your face to look more relaxed and self-assured, and showing the competition you are ready for whatever is up ahead, you will change how the mind approaches any conflicting situation and your potential results. This is true 10 out of every 10 times. Project a confident image of yourself and your

brain will gear up for confident thoughts which will create confident actions.

3. **Previewing your actions.** Doing things on pure instinct instead of having an idea of what would be the perfect way of doing them, are two completely different approaches to a circumstance but one can sometimes go right while the other will work out better much more often. Previewing your actions before doing them is similar to using visualizations but the difference is you will create the short mental image of what you want to do right before you do it. INSTANT IMAGE, INSTANT ACTION. Close your eyes for 1, 2, or 3 seconds, if time allows add a few more seconds and see yourself perform the action you are trying to accomplish and then open your eyes and perform this action in that instant. You will notice you are much more precise with your actions than ever before.

Remember, when meditating for mental toughness, you are going to practice the skills detailed above so that you can apply them under mentally tough conditions and overcome those challenges that others struggle with.

CHAPTER 11: MEDITATING FOR PROBLEM SOLVING

What does it mean to meditate for problem solving?

Well, if you have a problem, your brain could have the solution but when you're busy thinking about a million things and doing another 10 at the same time consciously or unconsciously, this will be impossible. By slowing down your thinking and calming your emotions through meditation and proper breathing techniques, it will be easier to focus on one problem at a time and find alternatives or possible solutions to fix the problem.

That's what meditation does best. It breaks things down to a simple idea or thought and concentrates only on this. These thoughts can be simply positive thoughts or ideas or they could be problems you need to find solutions for.

When you create a specific time to meditate, you are also creating time to solve a problem you are having which otherwise might not have a time dedicated to just it.

That's another positive result of meditating that most athletes never consider, and miss out on having any possibilities of finding alternatives to lifelong mistakes that are never corrected since they chose not to meditate.

What types of problems can I solve when meditating?

Any problem you might be having can be analyzed through the mind and sometimes you will find a solution immediately while other times it might take a lot longer or never at all. The brain has the capacity to find what you're looking for if you take the time to focus on it. The real problem occurs when you don't take the time to dedicate yourself to finding a solution and giving it the proper attention it deserves.

Why is meditating for problem solving important to me?

As an athlete, you are constantly being challenged and pushed which in turn means you are constantly being given new problems to solve every second, minute, or moment. By not preparing yourself to overcome these new challenges, you are allowing luck to become more valuable than your mental capacity to solve problems. This should never be the case. Remember, "Luck comes to those who are prepared". Be prepared to get lucky instead.

Five things to take into account when problem solving are:

1. Never overanalyze a problem to the point where it becomes a bigger problem than it really is.
2. Always allow the mind to try again when you don't find a solution instantly when meditating. You might

find a solution on the second or third time you meditate on the same problem.
3. Every problem has a solution. Meditating will help you search for a solution to a problem but keep in mind that you might need someone else's input to better solve it so always be humble enough to accept advise or to seek out help.
4. Not all problems need to be solved. If something is so minute in size that it does not deserve any attention, than skip it and move on to the important stuff that will cause the biggest impact in your results.
5. Meditating will help you solve many problems but sometimes visualizing will take you a step further, which is often necessary when you need to see mental images and mental videos of what's really going on.

Remember, meditating for problem solving is a great use for meditation but not the only use. Use your time wisely when meditating so that you make the most of it since the mind will give you the best quality concentration for a specific time interval and then the rest of the time will not be as productive and that's when you know you're done and need to end the session.

FINAL COMMENTS

Meditating is the next level of evolution for athletes. Physical training will continue to be the norm and new and better ways of training will keep coming around but the evolution of the mind will make the biggest and most impacting change in the years to come. Mentally enhanced athletes are the future and you can be in on it first or last, it's up to you. You decide! Get started and see the life changing effects meditation will have on you.

MORE TITLES BY THIS AUTHOR

The Ultimate Guide to Weight Training Nutrition: Maximize Your Potential

By Joseph Correa

Becoming Mentally Tougher In Bodybuilding by Using Meditation: Reach Your Potential by Controlling Your Inner Thoughts

By Joseph Correa

www.ingramcontent.com/pod-product-compliance
Lightning Source LLC
Chambersburg PA
CBHW070149080526
44586CB00015B/1903